THE NUTCRACKER

The Ballet Retold and Photographed by Ray Shaw

PRENTICE-HALL, INC.
ENGLEWOOD CLIFFS, NEW JERSEY

We are grateful
to The Chicago *Tribune* production
of "The Nutcracker"
for their cooperation in the
preparation of
this book.

Choreography and
Production Supervision by Ruth Page.

Production Design and Lighting
by Sam Leve.

Costumes by Rolf Gerard.

Photographs of Ruth Page's
International Ballet
taken in Chicago.

The Nutcracker
Retold and photographed by Ray Shaw

ISBN 0-13-627695-4
Library of Congress Catalog Card Number: 78-114686
Printed in the United States of America J
Prentice-Hall International, Inc., London
Prentice-Hall of Australia, Pty. Ltd., Sydney
Prentice-Hall of Canada, Ltd., Toronto
Prentice-Hall of India Private Ltd., New Delhi
Prentice-Hall of Japan, Inc., Tokyo

TO
FAITH
who loves ballet

There was great excitement in the home of Dr. and Mrs. Silberhouse. Tonight, as every Christmas Eve, they were having a big party. Their daughter Clara and her brother Fritz talked about it all day. They wondered what their godfather, Dr. Drosselmeyer, would bring. Last Christmas it had been gypsy dancers, the year before, waltzing horses. What would it be tonight?

No one else had such a clever godfather. Not only was he a doctor, but also an inventor and a marvelous magician.

Clara, excited and ready for the party to begin, was skipping down the hallway in her new party dress when she heard the doorbell ring. The guests were arriving! She ran to welcome her young friends.

"Come with me," she beckoned, leading them toward the drawing room.

Their parents followed, carrying gaily wrapped packages.

Clara's head began to spin as she watched her friends hop up and down, trying to see the Christmas tree. But a heavy curtain had been pulled across the glass-panelled doors.

"Oh, dear," sighed Clara. "What is happening to me?" She can see one cousin Henry, now two, sometimes three—— even five!

All at once the curtain swung back. The doors opened. The children's eyes grew wide. How beautiful! How exciting! So many presents!

The music rang out, and the parents began to dance.

With merry laughter, the children joined them.

There, at last, was Dr. Drosselmeyer in the doorway! Running to greet him, Clara felt hot and dizzy. She saw not one Godfather Drosselmeyer, but two, three, four, five. Will I have to do my homework five times every day? she wondered. Will I have to eat five bowls of Aunt Helga's lentil soup?

"You won't," said Dr. Drosselmeyer, as if she had spoken out loud.

"How are you, my dear Clara?" he asked, as he lightly touched her forehead. "You feel warm."

"Oh, no! I feel fine, thank you. Merry Christmas, Godfather," said Clara with a curtsy.

"And a Merry Christmas to you, my dear," he replied and went off to greet Dr. and Mrs. Silberhouse.

Then he raised his hands, and asked the guests for their attention. He unpacked two large dolls and wound them up with a key. Off they went into a lively, graceful dance. When the dance was over, the dolls collapsed gracefully and were put back into their boxes.

Next he wound up a soldier and a beautiful girl in blue who danced some fancy high-jump steps.

Everybody applauded.

Then Dr. Drosselmeyer waved his right arm, shook his wrist, and out of his sleeve came a bright, wooden figure with big twinkling eyes, a bushy beard, and large saw-like teeth. It looked like a soldier, but it wasn't! It was a funny little nutcracker.

All the children held out their hands.

But Dr. Drosselmeyer presented it to Clara.

This made Fritz angry. He snatched the nutcracker out of his sister's hand, threw it on the floor, kicked and stamped on it. Clara turned away in horror. She was afraid to look, afraid she might see five big brothers hurting five little nutcrackers.

Grabbing Fritz by the hair, Dr. Drosselmeyer led him to the door and ordered him out. Then the good doctor bandaged the injured nutcracker with his handkerchief and Clara gently placed it under the Christmas tree.

The music started again, and there was laughter and dancing. Grandfather and Grandmother led a dance and everyone joined in. Then Christmas Eve supper was served. Soon after eating, the children began to yawn and nod their heads. It was late! Time to go home.

With many thank-yous and Merry-Christmases, the guests left. And as it was very late the Silberhouse family went to bed. But Clara couldn't fall asleep.

She tiptoed into the living room to see how her nutcracker was feeling. Just then the clock began to strike. As Clara counted each stroke she felt someone near her. Strange shadows seemed to move along the wall.

They were mice! Big, ugly mice stealing toys and candy from under the tree.

Their leader had seven heads and wore a crown on each.
"What shall I do?" she cried, trembling with fear. A voice from under the tree caught her attention. There, at the head of an army of Fritz's toy soldiers stood the Nutcracker, giving commands.

A battle began. The soldiers fought bravely, but the enemy was strong and great in number.
Clara saw the King Mouse leap at the Nutcracker. "My poor, poor friend," she cried out. "How can I help you?" Suddenly she knew what to do! She took off her slipper and threw it with all her might at the monster king. He tripped. And as he fell, the Nutcracker, with a flash of his sword, killed him. The mice ran off in all directions when they saw their leader dead.

Kneeling, the Nutcracker thanked Clara for saving his life. As he rose she saw before her a handsome young prince.

"My name," he said, "is Halav Gavash. My father is a king. After my mother died, my father married a beautiful princess who really was a witch. She hated me, and wanted to get rid of me because she wanted her own son to be king some day."

One morning, the stepmother had said: "I shall cast a spell upon you. You will become a nutcracker! And you can be prince again only when you become chief of an army, go into battle and kill the commander of your enemy. But first a beautiful lady must fall in love with you. A tall order, isn't it, my dear stepson?" She let out a wicked laugh and disappeared into the woods.

"What a horrible woman!" cried Clara.

"Now I am grateful she turned me into a nutcracker. How else would I have met you, my dear Miss Silberhouse?" said the Prince, with a bow.

She curtsied in return. "Please call me Clara."

"Thank you," he answered. "And do call me 'Nutcracker.' I like the name."

"Where do you come from?" she asked. "Is it far away?"

"Not at all. Would you like to visit my kingdom?"

He took her hand, and as if by magic she found herself in a forest where the trees were covered with frosting, and snowflakes whirled and danced. The Snow Queen and her prince welcomed them with a ballet.

"Why is the water purple?" asked Clara, as they crossed a bridge of glazed orange peel.

"This is the River of Grape Juice," said the Prince.

In the distance they could see a castle made of peppermint sticks, licorice and caramels. "Now we are entering the Kingdom of Sweets," he told her.

"The beautiful lady you see is the Sugar Plum Fairy."

The Prince introduced Clara to the Court, and told them how she had saved his life. The Sugar Plum Fairy led them to a table of honor, high above a stage.

Angels circled the court.

While the two hungry guests were served, musicians and dancers entertained.

Spanish dancers clicked castanets in a dance called "Hot Chocolate."

Then a tall young man and a beautiful girl moved in the slow rhythm of an Arabian dance called "Coffee."

Next a rickshaw drew up.

Chinese dancers jumped out and danced the "Tea Dance."

A cake called "babka" was brought in, and the orchestra burst into a fast, lively song while Russian peasants whirled and stamped as fast as the musicians could play.

Clara and the Prince tasted almond candy while Marzipan Shepherdesses danced.

Then the Candy-box Lady, moving slowly across the floor, offered chocolates to Clara and the Prince.

Even the flowers came out to waltz for them, and bees and butterflies fluttered among the tulips, roses and cornflowers.

Clara and the Prince were delighted when the Sugar Plum Fairy herself danced for them.

And when the handsome Cavalier joined the Sugar Plum Fairy in a ballet, Clara was so busy watching them she forgot to eat her burnt-almond sundae with chocolate sauce.

The Sugar Plum Fairy and the Cavalier then invited Clara and the Prince to dance with them. And Clara, in her excitement, tripped and fell as she ran down the stairs to join them. When she looked up, there was Dr. Drosselmeyer at her side!

"Her fever is gone," he was whispering.

"May she have something to eat?" asked Mrs. Silberhouse.

"Of course! Anything she wants."

"Anything?" asked Clara. "Oh, then I'll finish my sundae."

"Sundae? You must have been dreaming, darling," smiled her mother.

"Dreaming? Oh, no! When the Nutcracker was fighting the mice, and I . . ."

"A nutcracker, my dear, isn't for fighting mice. It's for fighting nuts," laughed Dr. Drosselmeyer.

Clara grew quiet. She knew there was no use trying to tell them about her Nutcracker Prince. They wouldn't understand.

"I'm hungry," she said instead.